INTERIOR OF THE CHAMBER WHERE THE BÁB DECLARED HIS MISSION

# KHADÍJIH BAGUM

## The Wife of the Báb

by

H. M. BALYUZI

GR

GEORGE RONALD
OXFORD

GEORGE RONALD, Publisher

Softcover Edition 1982

Softcover Edition
ISBN 0-85398-101-9

# ILLUSTRATIONS

*'O well-beloved! ... Thou shalt not be a woman, like other women, if thou obeyest God in the Cause of Truth ...'*

The Báb

# FOREWORD

My father died on 12 February 1980. This publication commemorates the first anniversary of his passing.

Within a few weeks of his death the first volume of his projected four-volume work on the life of Bahá'u'lláh was published, with the title, *Bahá'u'lláh, The King of Glory.* The second volume was largely written, with only a few incompleted chapters, and this will be published. The format and contents of the third and fourth volumes had also been discussed, and the introduction to volume three written.

In November of the previous year he had suffered a heart attack. As he recovered from that illness, so he seemed to gain a physical strength such as had been denied him through many long years of crippling ill health. With this renewed vitality there came a surge of creative energy that saw him laying plans for several more books. Such was his eagerness to progress, that even whilst still in hospital recovering, he commenced a translation into Persian of his *Muḥammad and the Course of Islám*; he had by then completed a revision, this time written in Persian, of *Edward Granville Browne and the Bahá'í Faith,* incorporating much new material not included in the first, English-language version.

Further archival material was constantly being made available to him, stimulating him to still greater ambitions in the pursuit of Bahá'í scholarship, his great passion. His life of 'Abdu'l-Bahá he would rewrite, in a much expanded form to the present volume. Biographies of his kinsmen, members of the Afnán family, were planned, as was a biography of his father; all this, and much more. But it was not to be.

With the same suddenness that this new lease of life had been granted him, it was taken away, and his pen stilled. Yet it had not been in vain. For it was during these last four months of my father's life that he made his legacy to the Bahá'í World and, in so doing, sowed the seeds for the fruition of his most dear wish: that his work should continue and that the study of the history of the Faith should grow to its recognition as a major scholastic discipline.

In letters dated 10 November and 20 November 1979 he has left instructions that all his books and documents are to be kept together perpetually, 'for the benefit of all who seek knowledge', and that they are to form the nucleus of the 'Afnán Library', founded in the name of his father, Muvaqqari'd-Dawlih, and dedicated to Khadíjih Bagum, the wife of the Báb. Once established, the Library will be made available to all students and scholars wishing to research the history of the Faith.

It is his dedication of the Library to Khadíjih Bagum that lends to this small volume a special significance amongst my father's writings; for it testifies to his deep love and admiration for this noble soul. Khadíjih Bagum, through the lineage of her brother, Hájí Mírzá Abu'l-Qásim, was the great-aunt of Áqá Mírzá Hádí, the father of Shoghi Effendi, and likewise of my father's maternal grandfather and paternal grandmother, and also, through the lineage of her younger brother, Hájí Mírzá Siyyid Hasan (known as Afnán-i-Kabír—the Great Afnán), the aunt of his maternal grandmother. After the martyrdom of her Husband, Khadíjih Bagum removed to the house of the widow of Ḥájí Mírzá Siyyid 'Alí, the uncle who had reared the Báb from his infancy; and this house was close to the house in Shíráz where my grandfather was born and grew up. My grandfather would have related to my father how as a child he had played with Áqá Mírzá Hádí at the feet of Khadíjih Bagum, receiving instructions from her in the teachings of the Báb and of Bahá'u'lláh; and how later, as a young man, my grandfather came to act as amanuensis for the wife of the Báb, writing letters on her behalf to Bahá'u'lláh.

On hearing of the death in Karbilá of Fáṭimih Bagum, the mother of the Báb, my grandfather was sent by his uncle, Ḥájí Mírzá 'Abdu'lláh Khán, to that city, to attend to the affairs of his aunt, Bíbí Gawhar, who had remained with Fáṭimih Bagum ever since her departure from Shíráz. It was whilst he was thus absent from Shíráz that the death occurred of Khadíjih Bagum, and this sorrowful news was conveyed to him in a letter from Ḥájí Mírzá 'Abdu'lláh Khán in which he writes:

'What a grievous loss! What a heart-rending event! May God be my witness! She was a Princess of her Age, a rare gem in her Era, a saintly soul. In her lifetime, none could value her worth.'

Thus it is clear how, from his earliest years, my father would have come to share the reverence of his family for the wife of the Báb; and the reader will appreciate why this amongst all his unpublished writings was chosen to mark the first anniversary of his death.

In the forewords to his books my father always made sure that all who had assisted in their preparation and publication were acknowledged and thanked. Here I would beg the grace of all who helped with this booklet, in allowing me to defer my own thanks to a later occasion, so that I may the greater emphasize my boundless gratitude to one person, whose absolutely selfless devotion to the welfare of my father I have no means of adequately describing: his cousin, Abu'l-Qásim Afnán. The story told in this booklet is largely based on the written narrative of Abu'l-Qásim Afnán, the true custodian in this age of the traditions of the Afnán family. Suffice it to mention, as a small illustration, that much of the unique archival material which Abu'l-Qásim had in his possession, and which he unhesitatingly and without qualification made available to my father, he could equally readily have chosen to use himself in his own writings. No man could ever have desired a finer, truer friend.

Finally, it may prove useful if I refer the reader to two of my father's other books, *The Báb* and *Bahá'u'lláh, The King of Glory*. For in these are to be found many of the persons and incidents mentioned in this essay, but in their wider context. The reader's path may also be eased if, whilst reading the essay, reference is made to the Genealogy of the Báb prepared by the Guardian of the Faith, Shoghi Effendi, to be found in Nabíl's Narrative, *The Dawn-Breakers*.

*London*
*November 1980*

ROBERT BALYUZI

# KHADÍJIH BAGUM

## THE WIFE OF THE BÁB

# KHADÍJIH BAGUM

## The Wife of the Báb

In the long years after the martyrdom of the Báb, His wife, Khadíjih Bagum, would at times recount the story of her glorious but tragic life to the younger members of her family. Decades later, a niece, Maryam-Sulṭán Bagum, daughter of Ḥájí Mírzá Abu'l-Qásim, recalled all that she had heard from her saintly aunt; her grandson, Abu'l-Qásim Afnán, has now put on paper these recollections. Here is this invaluable account, in part purported to be a narration of Khadíjih Bagum herself.

The Báb and His wife were not widely separated in age. The house of Ḥájí Mírzá Siyyid 'Alí, the maternal uncle of the Báb—who became His guardian when His father died—and that of Mírzá 'Alí, the father of Khadíjih Bagum, adjoined each other; and so the Báb and Khadíjih Bagum were neighbours and playmates in their childhood. Mírzá Siyyid Ḥasan (the Great

1

Afnán of future years), a brother of Khadíjih Bagum, was about the same age. Whenever the children of the two households
came together to play, usually Siyyid 'Alí-
Muḥammad (the Báb) chose not to join in
their games, although He occasionally did,
and was always kind and considerate. Years
later, when Siyyid 'Alí-Muḥammad had
gone to Búshihr (Bushire), Khadíjih Bagum
had a vivid dream in which she saw her
young Cousin in a verdant plain, with
flowers in profusion, facing towards the
Qiblih (Mecca) in an attitude of prayer. He
wore a *labbádih* (an outer coat) on which
Qur'ánic verses were embroidered with
threads of gold. His face was radiant. She
related that dream to her mother, and to
the mother and grandmother of Siyyid 'Alí-
Muḥammad. They assured her that it was
her Cousin's assiduous attendance to His
prayers which had vouchsafed her that
splendorous vision. At this time Siyyid 'Alí-
Muḥammad could not have been more
than sixteen years old.

Still some years later, when Siyyid 'Alí-
Muḥammad had returned to Shíráz from
His visit to the holy cities of 'Iráq, Khadíjih

2

Bagum dreamt that Fáṭimih, the daughter of the Prophet Muḥammad, had come to ask for her hand in marriage to the Imám Ḥusayn.* Her mother, being told of this dream, rejoiced at the good fortune that awaited her daughter. That very day, Khadíjih Bagum recalled, the mother of Siyyid 'Alí-Muḥammad came to call on her mother, and His grandmother was also there. Whenever His grandmother came on a visit, Khadíjih Bagum stated, all would hurry to greet her, would kiss her shoulders, and then wait at the threshold of the room for her permission to enter and take a seat. Only Khadíjih Bagum's mother and the mother of Siyyid 'Alí-Muḥammad would at first be seated with her. And in her presence all would keep silent until she addressed them.

To continue the story of that day, so auspicious in her life, Khadíjih Bagum recounted: 'After they were all seated I took *sharbat* (a fruit syrup) to them and left the room. Then my sisters, one of whom was married to Ḥájí Mírzá Zaynu'l-'Ábidín†

---

* The martyred third Imám, who was a son of Fáṭimih.
† Her name was Zahrá Bagum; her husband was a

3

and the other to Ḥájí Mírzá Siyyid 'Alí,
came and went into the room. Not long
after, they all rose to go.' To Khadíjih
Bagum's surprise, the mother of Siyyid 'Alí-
Muḥammad kissed her on the forehead
before leaving. Seeing her puzzled look, her
mother hastened to explain: 'That kiss
implied that she has asked for your hand in
marriage to her Son. You see, the dream
you had last night has come true.' Khadíjih
Bagum, hearing the news and being re-
minded of her wondrous dream, was greatly
elated. The extraordinary respect and consideration which all the members of the
family gave to Siyyid 'Alí-Muḥammad,
and the accounts of His demeanour and
bearing which she had heard from her
elders, had already convinced Khadíjih
Bagum that her young Cousin stood head
and shoulders above them all. She recalled:
'From that day I felt a great stirring within
my heart. It seemed that the gate of God's
mercy and abundant bounty had been
flung open before my face. I felt immeasur-
ably proud of my coming union.'

cousin of the father of the Báb and great-grandfather of
Abu'l-Qásim Afnán.

4

Some two months passed before the wedding could be arranged. Marriage feasts were held in the house of Mírzá 'Alí, the father of Khadíjih Bagum, and in the house of the uncle of Siyyid 'Alí-Muhammad who had been His guardian. Shaykh Abú-Turáb, the Imám-Jum'ih of Shíráz, presided over the ceremony and read the usual oration. As it was customary for a relative of the bridegroom to respond, His uncle, Hájí Mírzá Siyyid 'Alí, accepted the suit. Later, the bride and the Groom were joined in wedlock in the house of Siyyid 'Alí-Muhammad Himself.*

Khadíjih Bagum recalled: 'His kindness towards me and His care for me were indescribable. He and His mother alike showered me with kindness and consideration.' The household in that small dwelling, destined to be the scene of the birth of a World Faith, consisted of the married couple, the mother of Siyyid 'Alí-Muhammad, and two black servitors: Fiddih, the woman, and Mubárak, the man.

Remembering those halcyon days preceding sorrows and suffering, Khadíjih

* The marriage took place in August 1842.

5

Bagum would say: 'No words can ever convey my wonderful feeling of good fortune.' But, not long after her marriage, she dreamt one night that a fearsome lion was standing in the courtyard of their house, and she herself had her arms round the neck of the lion. The beast dragged her twice round the whole perimeter of the courtyard, and once round half of it. She woke up, alarmed and trembling with fright, and related her dream to her Husband. His comment was: 'You awoke too soon. Your dream portends that our life together will not last more than two-and-a-half years.' K̲h̲adíjih Bagum was greatly distressed, but her Husband's affection and His words of comfort consoled her and prepared her to accept every adversity in the path of God.

Before long it was realized that K̲h̲adíjih Bagum was with child. And when the time came, her accouchement was exceedingly difficult and fraught with danger. Her mother-in-law reported to Siyyid 'Alí-Muḥammad that His wife was on the point of death. There lay a mirror beside Him, on which He wrote a prayer, and instructed His mother to hold the mirror in front of

His wife. That done, the child was safely delivered; but its life was short. Siyyid 'Alí-Muḥammad's mother was both grieved and angry. She remonstrated with her Son that if He had such powers, why had He not made an attempt to preserve the life of the child, and spare His wife so much suffering? Siyyid 'Alí-Muḥammad replied with a smile that He was not destined to leave any progeny, an answer which infuriated His mother; but to her reproaches He said no more.

The child, a son who was named Aḥmad by his Father, was buried under a cypress tree in the compound of the tomb of Bíbí-Dukhtarán.*

In the "Súratu'l-Qarába" (The Chapter of Kinship) of His mighty book, the *Qayyúm-u'l-Asmá'*, the Báb speaks of Aḥmad: 'O concourse of Light! Hear My call from the point of Fire in this ocean of snow-white water on this crimson earth. Verily, I am

* No one knows for certain who Bíbí-Dukhtarán was. It is said that she was a member of the Royal House of the Atábaks of Fárs—the Salghurids (1148–1270)—while others have claimed that since Bíbí-Dukhtarán means the Matron or the Mistress of the Maidens, it is possible that she was the Abbess of a Christian order of nuns.

God, besides Whom there is no other God.
On the exalted throne a beloved noble
woman, bearing the same name* as the
beloved of the First Friend,† was wedded to
this Great Remembrance;‡ and verily I
caused the angels of Heaven and the
denizens of Paradise, on the day of the
Covenant, to bear witness, in truth, to
God's Remembrance.

'O well-beloved! Value highly the grace
of the Great Remembrance, for it cometh
from God, the Loved One. Thou shalt not
be a woman, like other women, if thou
obeyest God in the Cause of Truth, the
greatest Truth. Know thou the great
bounty conferred upon thee by the Ancient
of Days, and take pride in being the consort
of the Well-Beloved, Who is loved by God,
the Greatest. Sufficient unto thee is this
glory which cometh unto thee from God,
the All-Wise, the All-Praised. Be patient in
all that God hath ordained concerning the
Báb and His Family. Verily, thy son,

*Khadíjih.
†The Prophet Muhammad.
‡The term 'Dhikr', here translated as 'Remembrance',
was frequently used by the Báb to refer to Himself.

8

Aḥmad, is with Fáṭimih,* the Sublime, in the sanctified Paradise.'

There is this further reference to Aḥmad in the "Súratu'l-'Abd" of the same mighty Book: 'All praise be to God Who bestowed upon the Solace of the Eyes,† in His youth, Aḥmad. We did verily raise him up unto God . . . O Solace of the Eyes! Be patient in what thy God hath ordained for thee. Verily He doeth whatsoever He willeth. He is the All-Wise in the exercise of His justice. He is thy Lord, the Ancient of Days, and praised be He in whatever He ordereth.'

During those years of their marriage, <u>Kh</u>adíjih Bagum related, her Husband had no definite occupation. He spent most of His time in the upper chamber of the house, engaged in devotions. At times, He went in the morning to His uncle's trading-house in the Saráy-i-Gumruk (Customs Serai). And some afternoons He would go for a walk in the fields outside the city and come home at

*The daughter of the Prophet Muḥammad.

†The Báb oftentimes refers to Himself in the *Qayyúm-u'l-Asmá'* as Qurratu'l-'Ayn—the Solace of the Eyes.

sunset. It was His wont to write His letters or His meditations in the early part of the evening, after performing the obligatory prayers pertaining to that period of the night.

Khadíjih Bagum recalled that one day in the late afternoon He came home earlier than usual. That evening, He said, He had a particular task to attend to, and asked that dinner be served earlier. Fiḍḍih, the servant who did the cooking, was so informed, and the family had their evening meal in the room of the mother of Siyyid 'Alí-Muḥammad. Then He retired for the night.

Speaking of the events of that memorable night, which, according to recollections of members of the Afnán family, occurred some time before the Báb declared His mission, Khadíjih Bagum related: 'An hour later, when the house was quiet and its occupants had gone to sleep, He rose from His bed and left the room. At first I took no particular notice of His absence, but when it lengthened to more than an hour I felt some concern. Then I went out to look for Him, but He was nowhere to be found.

ENTRANCE TO THE HOUSE OF THE BÁB IN S͟HÍRÁZ

WINDOWS OF THE BÁB'S LIVING QUARTERS OPENING ON THE COURTYARD

Perhaps, for some reason, He had left the house, I thought; but, trying the street door I found it locked from within, as usual. Then I walked to the western side of the house, looked up at the roof-top, and saw that the upper chamber was well lighted. This added to my surprise, because I had never known Him to go to that part of the house at that hour of the night, unless He had guests. And He always told me when a visitor was expected. He had not said that He was to have a guest that night. So, with both astonishment and trepidation, I went up the steps at the northern side of the courtyard. There I saw Him standing in that chamber, His hands raised heavenwards, intoning a prayer in a most melodious voice, with tears streaming down His face. And His face was luminous; rays of light radiated from it. He looked so majestic and resplendent that fear seized me, and I stood transfixed where I was, trembling uncontrollably. I could neither enter the room nor retrace my steps. My will-power was gone, and I was on the point of screaming, when He made a gesture with His blessed hands, telling me to go back.

This movement of His hands gave me back my courage, and I returned to my room and my bed. But all that night long I remained deeply disturbed. In my fitful moments of sleep that scene in the upper chamber would present itself to my mind, adding to my consternation. I kept asking myself what grave event had come to pass to evoke such sorrow and such tears, inducing prayer and supplication of such intensity. Sleep was impossible that night, and then came the dawn, so foreboding, and I heard the muezzin's call to prayer.

'At sunrise Fiḍḍih took the samovar and tea-things to the room of my mother-in-law and, as usual, He went to His mother's room to take tea. I followed Him there, and as soon as my eyes alighted on Him, that attitude and that majesty which I had witnessed the night before took shape before me. I paled and shuddered involuntarily. His mother had, at that moment, gone out of the room, and He was quietly drinking His tea. He raised His face to me, and received me with great kindness and affection, bidding me be seated. Then He passed to me what was left of the tea in His

12

own cup, which I drank. His kindness restored my courage, and when He asked me what it was that troubled me, I boldly replied that it was the change in Him which weighed heavily on my mind. "You are no longer", I told Him, "the same person I knew in our childhood. We grew up together, and we have been married for two years, living in this house, and now I see a different person before me. You have been transformed." I further remarked that this had made me anxious and uneasy. He smiled and said that although He had not wished to be seen by me in the condition of the previous night, God had ordained otherwise. "It was the will of God", He said, "that you should have seen Me in the way you did last night, so that no shadow of doubt should ever cross your mind, and you should come to know with absolute certitude that I am that Manifestation of God Whose advent has been expected for a thousand years. This light radiates from My heart and from My Being."* As soon as

* These are the words of the Báb as recalled by Khadíjih Bagum in later years, and recorded decades

I heard Him speak these words I believed in Him. I prostrated myself before Him and my heart became calm and assured. From that moment I lived only to serve Him, evanescent and self-effacing before Him, no thought of self ever intruding.'

The degree of Khadíjih Bagum's faith and the rank she attained are attested by Nabíl:* 'The wife of the Báb ... perceived at the earliest dawn of His Revelation the glory and uniqueness of His Mission and felt from the very beginning the intensity of its force. No one except Ṭáhirih, among the women of her generation, surpassed her in the spontaneous character of her devotion nor excelled the fervour of her faith.' In the prayer of visitation which Bahá'u'lláh revealed for Khadíjih Bagum after her death, He addresses her in these words: 'Thou art she, who, before the creation of the world of being, found the fragrance of the garment of the Merciful.'

---

after, and should not be taken as His exact words on that occasion. (Ed.)

*Nabíl-i-A'ẓam, *The Dawn-Breakers,* p. 191 (U.S. edn.).

Whenever Khadíjih Bagum spoke of the days of her marriage and the enforced separation from her Husband, and related the sufferings of the Báb, grief would so overwhelm her as to deprive her, for a while, of the power of speech. Her grief was felt and shared by all who heard her.

Not many months after His declaration to Mullá Husayn-i-Bushrú'í,* the Báb left Shíráz to go on pilgrimage to Mecca. The letter which He wrote to Khadíjih Bagum from Búshihr (the port of embarkation) shows His degree of attachment to her. His letter opened with these words: 'My sweet love, may God preserve thee.'

The return of the Báb from His pilgrimage to Mecca and Medina signalled the commencement of fierce denials and persecutions which reached their climax with the martyrdom of the Báb Himself. His wife's sufferings and agonies of mind and soul, although not under public gaze, can well be imagined. There was, for example, the

---

*The night of 22 May 1844.

15

incident of the raid by the emissaries of the Dárúghih (Chief Constable) of Shíráz, which she particularly recalled in later years:

'It was summer-time in the month of Ramadán. We slept on the roof, and my mother-in-law slept in the courtyard. *Farráshes** of the Governor made their way to our home from a neighbour's roof. That Blessed Being rose up and told me to go downstairs. The intruders took away every book and every piece of writing that they found in the upper chamber. To Him they said, "You have to come with us to the house of 'Abdu'l-Hamíd Khán (the Dárúghih)." Down below, I could hear Him expostulating with the *farráshes,* demanding to know why they had broken into and forced their way into our house, in the dead of night. "It has been reported to us", they replied, "that some people have assembled in this house." Since they had by then discovered the untruth of the report, He asked if they would now go away in peace. But they were not satisfied and took Him away. God knows what His mother and I

* Footman, lictor, attendant.

16

suffered that night. We were thankful that His grandmother, an elderly lady, was not there. It was close to dawn when He came home. They had demanded money and, as He had no cash with Him, they had laid hands on the cashmere shawl round His waist and cut it up. 'Abdu'l-Ḥamíd Khán had kept half of the shawl for himself.'

Ḥájí Mírzá Abu'l-Qásim, a brother of Khadíjih Bagum, wrote the full story of that night in a letter to Ḥájí Mírzá Siyyid Muḥammad, a maternal uncle of the Báb, who at that time resided in Búshihr. This letter is extant.

Not long after that night when the privacy of His home had been stealthily invaded, the authorities arrested the Báb and detained Him, under lock and key, in the house of the Dárúghih. And it was rumoured in the city that he would be put to death in the same house. Ḥájí Mírzá Siyyid 'Alí, the uncle of the Báb who had been His guardian in His childhood, did his utmost to provide comfort and relief. He himself had been beaten up and was ailing, yet he was ceaseless in his efforts. And so was the sister of Khadíjih Bagum, whose name was Zahrá Bagum. At this time, when no male member of the family dared come to their house, Khadíjih Bagum recalled, it was only her sister who would come, dressed as a beggar. The famous mosque of Shíráz, known as Masjid-i-Naw (the New Mosque), was close by. Here, in a secluded spot in the mosque, her sister would change her own *chádur** for one tattered and patched, and would then go to the house of the Báb to bring any news there was of Him to His mother.

Amongst the notables of Shíráz, the one man ever ready to render assistance was Shaykh Abú-Turáb, the Imám-Jum'ih. Zahrá Bagum, together with the wife of Hájí Abu'l-Hasan-i-Bazzáz (the Mercer),†

---

*An outer garment which envelops a woman from head to foot, like a sack.

† Hájí Abu'l-Hasan was a fellow-pilgrim of the Báb, on the boat that took them from Búshihr to Jiddah. He was greatly impressed by the mien and bearing of Siyyid 'Alí-Muhammad, his fellow-townsman. Later, in Shíráz, he learned of the claim and the mission of Siyyid 'Alí-Muhammad, the Báb, and gave Him his unswerving allegiance, which never faltered in the face of life-long persecution. Many were the hardships that he bore resolutely in His path and for His sake. Hájí Abu'l-Hasan

who was closely related to the Imám-
Jum'ih, visited regularly the house of this
benevolent divine to obtain news and seek
his intercession on behalf of the Báb. The
Imám-Jum'ih would reply that he was
powerless in the face of the open and
relentless enmity of their own relative, and
his advice was to try and calm down that
vociferous man. He was referring to Ḥájí
'Abdu'l-Ḥusayn, a brother of the wife of
Ḥájí Mírzá Siyyid Muḥammad, who was
foremost in denouncing, insulting, and per-
secuting the Báb. But when the divines of
Shíráz passed the verdict of death on the
Báb, and had their infamous sentence
confirmed by Ḥusayn Khán, the Niẓamu'd-
Dawlih and Governor-General of the province of Fárs, the Imám-Jum'ih refused to
add his signature to theirs. Three of those
divines—Shaykh Ḥusayn, the Náẓimu'sh-
Sharí'ah (known as Ẓálim, the Tyrant),
Shaykh Mihdíy-i-Kujúrí, and Shaykh
Muḥammad-'Alíy-i-Maḥalláti—presented
themselves at the house of the Imám-

---

was the father of Mírzá Muḥammad-Báqir Khán
Dihqán, a distinguished and greatly devoted Bahá'í of
the period which covered the Ministry of 'Abdu'l-Bahá.

19

Jum'ih in an effort to win him over to their side. <u>Shaykh</u> Abú-Turáb rejected their plea, censured their reprehensible conduct, and turned them out of his house. By now Zahrá Bagum, the mother of the Báb, and the wife of Hájí Abu'l-Hasan had together persuaded the Imám-Jum'ih to find a way out of the impasse. And so, as well as declining to be associated with the death verdict pronounced by the divines, he made them agree to summon the Báb to Masjid-i-Vakíl (the Vakíl's Mosque),* and there give Him the chance to repudiate His claim. One day, heralds were sent through the streets to call, in the name of the Governor, on the people of <u>Sh</u>íráz to assemble, in the afternoon of a certain Friday, in Vakíl's Mosque to hear the Bab's recantation.

And now to continue with <u>Kh</u>adíjih Bagum's recollections: 'We were all apprehensive lest something untoward should happen, but it was being said that once He had declared His repentance, He would be allowed to come home. This was comforting to us. On that Friday afternoon, we wished

*It was built by Karím <u>Kh</u>án-i-Vakíl (reigned 1750–79), the founder of the short-lived Zand dynasty.

to send a woman to the mosque, to bring us news of the happenings there. But it was found to be impossible. Women were not admitted. However, news was brought to us that *farráshes* had taken Him to the mosque, where He had ascended the pulpit and spoken words which had kindled once again the wrath of the Governor and the divines, whereupon they had led Him back to confinement. Soon after, a cholera epidemic suddenly struck Shíráz, taking a heavy toll of lives. The people fled from the city and very few were left behind.

'One day, to our indescribable joy, He came home and stayed two or three days. Only Ḥájí Mírzá Siyyid 'Alí and two others of the believers knew of His release. But these were the last days of my life with Him. A few days before the arrival of the month of Ramaḍán, He announced that His sojourn in Shíráz was no longer advisable and that He would leave the city that very night. We, who had known how much He had suffered in Shíráz, were happy and contented that He could now reach a place of safety. In the afternoon He called on Ḥájí Mírzá Siyyid 'Alí and Ḥájí Mírzá Zaynu'l-

'Ábidín and his wife, who was my sister, to bid them farewell, returned home about sunset, and two hours later, all alone, left the house. His clothes and the necessities for the journey had been sent out of the city earlier. Accompanied by one of the believers He took the road to Iṣfahán.*

'Now, we were most of the time in the house of Ḥájí Mírzá Siyyid 'Alí, expecting the arrival, any minute, of a messenger with news of Him. The cholera epidemic was over and the Governor had returned to Shíráz. As soon as Ḥusayn Khán was back, he sent his *farráshes* to seek Him. We pleaded ignorance of His whereabouts. 'Abdu'l-Ḥamíd Khán, the Dárúghih, who had on his own authority allowed Him to depart from Shíráz, likewise denied having any knowledge of His destination. Then the *farráshes* of the Governor came to arrest my brother, Ḥájí Mírzá Abu'l-Qásim, who was ill in bed and unable to walk. So they threw him over their shoulders and carried him to

*In the last days of September 1846. A somewhat different account of this episode is given in Browne (ed.), *A Traveler's Narrative*, p. 9 (U.S. edn.), and *The Dawn-Breakers*, pp. 197–8 (U.S. edn.).

the residence of the Governor. Of course he knew nothing, but Ḥusayn Khán would not believe him, and began to remonstrate so vehemently that my brother could not withstand that torrent of abuse and lost consciousness. Indeed, he was driven almost to the point of death. Finally, Ḥusayn Khan told him that he should produce his Brother-in-Law within fifteen days or pay a fine of 15,000 túmáns.* Whatever my brother said had no effect on the cruel Governor. Then Ḥájí Muḥammad-Ṣádiq-i-Iṣfahání, a friend and business associate of my brother, intervened to stand surety for him. The Governor's men once again hoisted Ḥájí Mírzá Abu'l-Qásim on to their shoulders and brought him home. He was thrown unceremoniously into the forecourt of the house and abandoned there. God knows what my brother and we went through during those two or three hours. One result of this ill-treatment was an affliction of the eyes. The pain was severe and my brother could not open his eyes, whilst tears streamed from them the whole time.

*A substantial sum in those days.

'Upon the expiration of fifteen days, the *farráshes* came again. They would not allow my brother even to mount his donkey, but took him away in the same manner as before. God be praised that just as Ḥusayn Khán was demanding menacingly his 15,000 túmáns from Ḥájí Muḥammad-Ṣádiq and my brother, a letter was brought to him from the Governor of Iṣfahán, Manúchihr Khán, who had written that the Person whom Ḥusayn Khán was seeking was in Iṣfahán, an honoured Guest of the Governor himself, and that no member of His family should be molested in any way. Ḥusayn Khán had perforce to moderate his demand, and exacted 1,500 túmáns instead. The Farrásh-Báshí (Chief of the *farráshes*) and his men all demanded money and had to be satisfied.'

Ḥájí Mírzá Ḥasan-'Alí, a younger brother of Ḥájí Mírzá Siyyid 'Alí, lived in Yazd. Once every few months he would send a messenger to Shíráz with a letter for his sister, the mother of the Báb, to console and comfort her, and give her whatever news he had of the Báb. At times there was a letter from the Báb Himself, addressed to

24

His wife, mother and grandmother. Ḥájí Mírzá Siyyid Ḥasan (later known as Afnán-i-Kabír), a brother of Khadíjih Bagum, was in Iṣfahán during those years, but he never wrote to her a line about her Husband. Indeed, at that time Ḥájí Mírzá Siyyid Ḥasan was hostile to his Kinsman, the Báb.*

And now to continue with Khadíjih Bagum's recollections: 'Then Ḥájí Mírzá Siyyid 'Alí left for Yazd. Of the young members of the family, Ḥájí Mírzá Javád† and Ḥájí Mírzá Muḥammad-'Alí‡ came to see us oftentimes and provided us with our means of livelihood. They were exceedingly kind. Whenever they met my mother-in-law, they invariably kissed her hand and spoke such words as would bring her peace of mind.

'A few months passed, until news reached us that He, the Qá'im of the House of

---

*A half-brother of Khadíjih Bagum, Ḥájí Muḥam-mad-Mihdí—a poet of distinction whose soubriquet was Ḥijáb, had gone to Bombay for commercial pursuits.
† Son of Ḥájí Mírzá Siyyid 'Alí.
‡ Son of Ḥájí Mírzá Siyyid Muḥammad.

25

Muḥammad, had been taken to Ṭihrán,*
and then to Tabríz. These fragmentary
pieces of news caused us great distress. My
mother-in-law appealed to her brother,
Ḥájí Mírzá Siyyid 'Alí, to do something.
Thus it was that he went from Yazd to
Chihriq, and in the end met a martyr's
death in Ṭihrán.

'Ḥájí Mírzá Siyyid 'Alí's martyrdom in
Ṭihrán, and the martyrdom of that Blessed
Person [the Báb] in Tabríz were concealed
from the women of the family, and whenever we mentioned rumours that had come
to our ears, the men would hotly deny
them—all lies they would say.'

Of course the men of the family knew what
had happened. Even before those dire
events had come to pass, Ḥájí Mírzá Abu'l-
Qásim, the brother of Khadíjih Bagum, had
found it impossible to stay in Shíráz, and
had taken Mírzá Javád, the eighteen-year-
old son of Ḥájí Mírzá Siyyid 'Alí, with him
to go on pilgrimage to Mecca. Mírzá Javád

* Although summoned by the Sháh to Ṭihrán, an order
from the Prime Minister countermanded this, when the
Báb was within thirty miles of the capital. (Ed.)

THE UPPER CHAMBER WHERE THE BÁB DECLARED HIS MISSION

A LETTER OF THE BÁB TO HIS WIFE

had, only a year before, married his cousin,
Khadíjih Sulṭán-Bagum, a daughter of Ḥájí
Mírzá Siyyid Muḥammad. On the way
back, the youthful Mírzá Javád (now a
Ḥájí) fell ill and died at Jiddah, where he
was buried.* Ḥájí Mírzá Abu'l-Qásim, now
alone, visited the holy shrines of 'Iráq
before returning home. More than a year
had passed since the martyrdom of the Báb
and that of His uncle, when Ḥájí Mírzá
Abu'l-Qásim reached home with the sad
news of the death of Ḥájí Mírzá Javád. The
announcement of this youth's lamentable
death perforce revealed the fact that his
father was dead, too—cruelly beheaded in
Ṭihrán. And the martyrdom of the Báb
Himself could no longer be kept a secret.
Now, all three were mourned together.

The mother of the Báb was inconsolable.
The spiteful attitude and the lashing,
wounding tongues of some members of the
family, who were still bitterly hostile, inten-

---

*A receipt exists, from a reciter of the Qur'án in
Karbilá, which lists the clothing and other belongings of
Ḥájí Mírzá Javád. They had been given to him by Ḥájí
Mírzá Abu'l-Qásim, and in return, he was to recite in
public verses of the Qur'án on behalf of the deceased.

sified her agonies, until she could not bear
any longer the injuries inflicted upon her
and decided to take herself away from
Shíráz. At first she wished to go to Mash-
had—the most sacred city of Írán, where
the remains of the Eighth Imám, 'Alí Ibn
Musa'r-Riḍá, repose—and have her mother
with her. But she changed her mind, leased
the house of the Báb to Mírzá Muḥammad-
Ḥusayn-i-Bazzáz, and, accompanied by
Bíbí Gawhar*—a half-sister of Ḥájí Mírzá
'Abdu'lláh Khán-i-Bályúz—and Ḥájí Mubárak, the faithful black servant of the Báb,
went to Karbilá and resided there for the
rest of her life. Later, Mírzá 'Abdu'l-Majíd
and his wife, both believers, went to live in
the same holy city. The wife of Mírzá
'Abdu'l-Majíd served the mother of the Báb
with exemplary devotion.

Khadíjih Bagum, recalling those days of
desolation and distress, would say: 'Her
departure from Shíráz added greatly to my
burden of sorrow and deepened the sadness
of my heart. I had no longer by my side a
comforter whose love and sympathy and
care had sustained me over the years. I went

* A great-aunt of the present writer.

28

to live with my sister, the widow of Ḥájí Mírzá Siyyid 'Alí. She herself had lost both her husband and her only son within the space of one year. As great as was my sorrow, hers was even greater and I had to comfort her. The loyal, faithful Fiḍḍih was with me.

'Of the servants and the maids whom we had in the house, no one knew of the martyrdom of that Blessed Being and the martyrdom of His uncle. It was not possible to talk of such matters with anyone. In Karbilá, Ḥájí Mubárak had purchased a broom with a green handle to sweep every day the courtyard of the Shrine of Imám Ḥusayn. Since green is the colour of the House of Muḥammad, Ḥájí Mubárak meant to keep alive the hope that one day he would see again, with his own eyes, the luminous face of his beloved Master in this world. In Shíráz we told Fiḍḍih and others that the Master and His uncle had gone to Bombay for the purposes of trade. When our house was being repaired Fiḍḍih was so happy, saying all the time that the Master was on His way home, and the house was being repaired in preparation for His homecoming. The joy of this faithful soul was wonderful to behold and truly overwhelming. We were all deeply affected.

'When the captives of Nayríz and Zanján were brought to Shíráz, they could not approach us nor could we approach them. But after a while the daughters of Ḥujjat and some ladies from Nayríz visited us in the house of Ḥájí Mírzá Siyyid 'Alí. Thereafter we were able to visit one another.

'Years passed, and Mírzá Áqá* grew up. He was greatly attached to me. The Blessed Beauty [Bahá'u'lláh] was in Baghdád. Mírzá Áqá wrote to Him on my behalf and I was honoured with a reply. Then came a day when Mullá Muḥammad-i-Zarandí, Nabíl-i-A'ẓam, travelled to Shíráz with a mandate from the Blessed Beauty to announce His Mission to the People of the Bayan† in this city. In the house of Mírzá Áqá he told the believers gathered there that the Promised One of the Bayán had come, and they, one and all, pledged their loyalty. One day I asked him to come. I was

* The son of Ḥájí Mírzá Zaynu'l-'Ábidín and Zahrá Bagum, sister of Khadíjih Bagum.
† Followers of the Báb.

behind a curtain, and as soon as I heard him say that the Blessed Beauty was "He Whom God shall manifest", promised in the *Bayán,* I experienced the same feeling as I had that night, standing at the threshold of the upper chamber of our home, and became certain that what God had promised for the "Year Nine" had come to pass. I immediately put my forehead on the ground in adoration and thanksgiving. Then, I could only whisper: "Offer at His sacred threshold my most humble devotion." I did not hesitate for a moment and my submission was instantaneous and total.

'Again, years passed, and one day a letter came from Mírzá Muḥammad-Ḥasan, who lived in Iṣfahán, announcing that Áqá Siyyid Yaḥyá and his sister,* accompanied by Shaykh Salmán,† were coming to Shíráz on their way to the Holy Land. Believers travelling to Shíráz always came to pay me a visit and I received them in the home of Mírzá Áqá, my nephew. Women amongst the believers in Shíráz, who were

---

* Munírih Khánum, who was to become the wife of 'Abdu'l-Bahá.

† The celebrated courier of Bahá'u'lláh.

few in number, used to call at the house of
Hájí Mírzá Siyyid 'Alí to see me. I lived in
that house and had it prepared to receive the
travellers from Iṣfahán. But I heard that on
their arrival they had gone to the house of
Hájí Mírzá Siyyid Muḥammad, which was
close by. I went there myself and brought
them to this house. My nephew, Hájí Siyyid
'Alí,* was also in Shíráz at this time. They
stayed for fifteen days, and those were some
of the happiest days of my life.'

Here ends the story of Khadíjih Bagum, as
told by her to the young members of her
family.

Shaykh Salmán visited Shíráz often, and
whenever he came from 'Akká, he brought
a Tablet from Bahá'u'lláh addressed to
Khadíjih Bagum, and presents and tokens
as well. Once he brought her a book in the
handwriting of Zaynu'l-Muqarrabín—a
gift from Bahá'u'lláh; another time a ring
and shirts which Bahá'u'lláh had worn,
with handkerchiefs and turban-cloths used
round His *táj*—His headgear.

* The son of Hájí Mírzá Siyyid Ḥasan.

Munírih Khánum carried to the presence of Bahá'u'lláh three requests from Khadíjih Bagum. She longed for the house of her Husband to be repaired so that she might live there. She asked for the hand of Furúghíyyih Khánum, a daughter of Bahá'u'lláh, on behalf of her nephew, Hájí Siyyid 'Alí. And she begged for permission to travel to 'Akká and have the bounty of attaining the presence of her Lord, in Whose path her Husband had gladly offered His life. Bahá'u'lláh granted all her requests. The house of the Báb received the repairs needed, and Khadíjih Bagum transferred her residence there. But, before long, the succession of visitors to that house aroused the wrath of the adversaries. Hájí Farhád Mírzá, the Mu'tamidu'd-Dawlih, an uncle of Násiri'd-Dín Sháh, who, at the time, was Governor-General of the province of Fárs, decided to have the house demolished. Mírzá Abu'l-Hasan, the Munshí-Báshí (Chief Secretary), and Mírzá Zaynu'l-'Ábidín Khán-i-'Alí-Ábádí, both of whom were Bahá'ís and members of the retinue of the Prince-Governor, close to his person, managed to avert that catastrophe.

For a while Khadíjih Bagum had to live once again in the house of her sister, but eventually returned to the house of her Husband.

As for her second request, the marriage of her nephew to Bahá'u'lláh's daughter was to cause Khadíjih Bagum untold sorrow. For Hájí Siyyid 'Alí had promised her, should her request be granted and he be accepted as Bahá'u'lláh's son-in-law, that he would come from Yazd, where he resided and traded, and would take Khadíjih Bagum with him to the Holy Land, that her eager desire to attain the presence of Bahá'u'lláh might be fulfilled. But when news of Bahá'u'lláh's consent to the marriage was received, this fickle nephew broke his promise and sent word that conditions prevented his coming to Shíráz, and that he was proceeding to the Holy Land via 'Ishqábád and hoped to arrange for her journey as soon as he could. Khadíjih Bagum sensed that her chance to travel to the Holy Land was now gone forever; in those days a woman travelled only in the company of a close relative and such opportunities were rare.

Khadíjih Bagum was heart-broken. Her health deteriorated and despite the attentions of several physicians, within two months of the receipt of that distressing intelligence, she passed away in the house of her glorious Husband, three hours before sunset on Monday, 2 Dhi'l-Qi'dih 1299 A.H. (15 September 1882). And strangely, the faithful servitor, Fiḍḍih, died two hours after the death of her mistress, in the same house. As her brother, Ḥájí Mírzá Abu'l-Qásim, has recorded, Khadíjih Bagum's body was taken that night to the public bath, known as Ḥammám-i-Guldastih, which was adjacent to the Masjid-i-Naw, to be washed and prepared for interment. That same night she was buried within the Shrine of Sháh-Chirágh,* in the section known as Ṣadru'l-Ḥifáẓ. Fiḍḍih, too, was buried within that Shrine in a chamber facing the Ṣadru'l-Ḥifáẓ (to the north of the tomb of Mír Siyyid Aḥmad), which was called Masjid-i-Zanánih (Women's Mosque).

* The tomb of Mír Siyyid Aḥmad, a son of the Seventh Imám, Músa'l-Káẓim.

www.ingramcontent.com/pod-product-compliance
Lightning Source LLC
Chambersburg PA
CBHW021226020426
42331CB00003B/481